Book Endorse

MW00622489

"Louada has written an honest, gut-wrenching life story as she shines the light on the heart-breaking past of a little girl trapped in a world of alcoholism, abuse, rejection, fear and neglect. Today she is a powerful, anointed, loving and forgiving minister of the gospel. While sharing her life, in hopes of helping others, she always points one to Jesus for healing and redemption. In this book you will find hope and help for your own life."

–Carol Torrance, U.S. National Director, S.C. Region Aglow International

"I almost couldn't breathe as I read about Louada, the little girl in a runaway car, awakened by an angel. What a beautiful testimony of the redemptive power of Jesus! He really does save, heal, and deliver to the uttermost. This book will bring glory to the Lord and healing for many. Well Done!"

–Cindy Danielson, Core Leadership Team,
Impact Christian Fellowship, Kerrville, TX

"My heart was wonderfully and tenderly warmed as I read my friend's touching story of God's REDEEMING LOVE. In this fast-paced recounting of finding her 'Father,' Louada brings a comforting word of hope for those marginalized because of a sinful, fallen humanity. She beautifully carries the reader through the struggles that she faced being separated from God and the consequences of fallen people. Highly recommended for your encouragement."

–Michael Cave, Executive Director, Commission and Ministers Network

"Everyone loves a hero, as long as it is someone else. Heroes are broken, bruised, scarred, and torn, but the experience transforms them into conquering warriors. As Paul the Apostle stated, 'Tribulation works patience; and patience, experience...' (Romans 5:3-4). Louada Raschke invites you on her very personal and honest experience—from victim to victor; from conquered to conqueror; from fear to faith. You will laugh. You will cry. You. Will. Be. Changed.

Join Louada on her journey with this miracle-working Jesus and allow Him to transform you into the hero He destined you to be."

–Roberta J. (Bertie) Jones, MD

"This is a must-read for those wanting proof that our Creator-God works through our lives to protect and restore His kids. Louada writes with vulnerable simplicity to paint a portrait of Father God's faithfulness. Be ready to be inspired to take a step of faith as you walk this life's sacred journey."

–Jack & Carol Rothenflue, authors and retired pastors to missionaries

"It is a joy for me to recommend this wonderful book written by Louada Raschke, with Dr. Sandy Kirk, about the life and ministry of my friend and sister in Christ. She is a woman whose heart burns with passion for God and compassion for people, especially those who are hurting. She is willing to be vulnerable and allow her story to be told so that others going through painful, hopeless situations may know there is a Heavenly Father who sees, loves, and transforms."

–Elizabeth Brown, President, Central TX Area Aglow Int'l

"LOUADA is an amazing book about an amazing woman! Louada, the woman, is living proof that God does indeed call women to ministry in a mighty way. Without assuming anything, Louada is a standard bearer for women in ministry all over the world. Perhaps her struggle from abuse, heartache, poverty and loneliness was the crucible that produced the minister we see and enjoy today. So gifted, so talented! And Louada, the woman, is a friend indeed. She is a joy to be around. Her cup is always full. Without the pride and arrogance that so frequently captures God's gifted ministers, Louada is always just Louada, a friend indeed. For those who have suffered various kinds of abuse in life, this book offers the hope that is in Jesus, the Christ, our living Lord and Savior. What Louada describes is available to the hurting around the world. God is no respecter of persons. What He did for Louada, He will do for you.

You can be rid of the heartache and pain that clings to you from abuse and pain that happens to all humanity. The secret: Believe! Believe Louada's testimony. Believe that God loves you just as He loves Louada and her family. Believe! Never stop believing!

"When our father in the faith, Abraham, took his son Isaac to the mountain to sacrifice him, he never stopped believing that God was even able to raise him from the dead. He is our father in the faith and a testimony to the grace and love of God. In her book, Louada brings that message to us, loud and clear. I encourage you to read every word. If your life mirrors some of her challenges and sorrows, put her testimony to work in your life. With faith, you can have that same LIFE living in you. Open your heart to this wonderful Savior that Louada shows us in living color. Receive from Him, just as Louada tells us. Like the old hymn, 'What He has done for others, He will do for you.'"

–Rene Brown, President, Foundation Ministries

"I have known Louada Raschke for more than a decade. From the first moment I met her at The Coming King Sculpture Prayer Garden in Kerrville, TX, I could tell she was radically in love with Jesus. I always enjoy meeting people who are 'on-fire' for the LORD. They are different, like the ones with the flames over their heads in the upper room. They are the ones who get to do God's stuff... the fun stuff and the hard stuff. God trusts them to do His work on this earth. Their calling is their passion and the focus of their lives. Louada is one of those 'hair on-fire' Christians. She is the real deal.

"Without God's protection and intervention, Louada could not have lived through her painful past. However, the LORD had a plan to use this lady to reach thousands with His message of healing, deliverance and love. She is walking-talking proof that God can use a damaged life to set others on the path to freedom and joy. Since 1989, when Sherry and I prayed for the 'Baptism of the Holy Spirit' empowerment as young Southern Baptists, God has used us to help set the captives free. Over the years, psychiatrists and psychologists have called us for help with their patients who could not be helped with traditional medical treatments. God is using

Louada Raschke in the same way, to distribute supernatural healing and deliverance to many.

"I have heard it said: 'Don't trust any Christian who doesn't limp.' The trials and tragedies of this life have a way of making a believer humble and useable to the LORD. The Holy Spirt anointing on Louada Raschke can change your life for the better. I pray her testimony will inspire and heal you, in the mighty name of Jesus. AMEN."

–Max Greiner, Jr., Max Greiner, Jr. Designs, The Coming King Foundation

Louada

Louada

Never, Never Give Up!

A Stunning Triumph of Hope

Rev. Louada Raschke

with Sandy D. Kirk, PhD

ISBN (paperback): 978-1-7351221-4-4

ISBN (e-book): 978-1-7351221-6-8

Design by: Christy Day, Constellation Book Services

Published by Louada Raschke Publications

Website: www.Louada.org

DEDICATION

This book is dedicated to my "daddy," Jack Turner. You are by far the greatest man I have ever known. The day you came into mine and momma's life, everything changed for the better. You rescued us! How I thank the Lord for you.

My beautiful daughter Diona Montgomery—you are spunky, fiery, loyal. I love your strong sense of justice. You are a defender and protector of the weak and hurting. God has given you a prophetic edge and discernment. In one of my most difficult seasons, you comforted me, took care of me, and stood with me. You bring me such great joy! You are my precious daughter, and you are also my friend.

My son-in-law Sean—actually you are my son-in-"love." I am forever grateful God brought you into our family. I enjoy your easygoing personality. You are a wonderful husband to my daughter and father to my grandchildren. Thank you for working so hard to care for and provide for them. You are a blessing!

My grandson Zayne—you are considerate and kindhearted like no other. You notice those around you and are sensitive to their needs. You have a beautiful, pure servant's heart, willing to help wherever you can. You are inquisitive, smart, funny, and of course, handsome!

I so love your gentle, sweet spirit and personality!

My granddaughter Emma—you are a mix of sweet and spunky like your mom! You can do anything you set your mind to. You are very perceptive and don't miss a thing. You are gorgeous, opinionated, fearless, intelligent. You are thoughtful and loving. Life is not boring when you are around! I love who you are!

Last but not least by any means, my son Cameron Raschke—you are an overcomer who not only defied all the odds and all the doctors' diagnoses but annihilated and far exceeded them! God gifted you with a brilliant mind, tenacity, and endurance. You have an entrepreneurial spirit. You think big. You are a strong, good-looking, successful young man. Most of all, you have a compassionate, gentle heart and want to help people. I love our relationship. I love our talks.

I love each of you more than you will ever know. I could not imagine my life without you in it. I am blessed beyond measure.

CONTENTS

Foreword   *xiii*

Preface   *xvii*

1: One Terrifying Night   1

2: My Broken Momma   7

3: A Little Girl Finds a Dad   13

4: Baptized in the Holy Spirit   23

5: Bold as a Lion   29

6: My Hidden Shame and Pain   35

7: Forgiving the Unforgivable   43

8: Chipping Away at the Mountain   49

9: Life's Unexpected Interruptions   57

10: God's Rescue Mission   65

11: Never Give Up on Your Calling   75

Acknowledgments   *79*

Appendix   *87*

Pictures of My Family   *90*

Foreword

by Sandy D. Kirk, PhD

I walked into the room full of Aglow International women. Because I would be moving to this new town in the hill country of Texas, I prayed, "Lord, please let me have at least one divine appointment."

Suddenly, I heard a shrill voice crying out, "Oh, my gosh! Dr. Sandy, I read your book. I loved it!"[1] I could hardly believe the Lord would give me such a quick answer to prayer. The lady's name was Louada, and she was the worship leader. Because of Louada's bombastic introduction, now everyone wanted to meet me. I didn't have one divine appointment; I probably had at least 50!

Nothing means more to me than for someone to read one of my books about the cross and the Father's cup, and from that day forward our hearts were knit together. We decided to join our ministries to plan a retreat, and I want you to know, I was blown away by this amazing worship leader and powerful speaker of the Gospel.

Now I can tell you that I have stood beside her as she laid hands on hurting people and they were overwhelmed with the power of the Holy Spirit. I have seen people weep in her arms as the love of Jesus flows through her. I have stood in a crowd of worshippers as she led us in worship and took us places in God I had never been before.

Then I heard her preach on the mountain at The Coming King Sculpture Prayer Garden outside of Kerrville, Texas. I wept as I heard her preach the cross with burning lips and blazing heart (see Chapter 10). I know her message brought Jesus, the Lamb who was slain, the reward of His suffering.

To see her minister, you would never know the incredible abuse she experienced as a child. That's why her story will give you hope. You may have felt the mountains before you were too high to climb. Or perhaps you have felt that your past is too scarred with pain to fully break free. Read Louada's story, and you will discover the secret of how to chisel and smash down those mountains with God's Word.

You will find how to walk through the valley of the shadow of death with grace and faith. You will learn how to forgive the unforgivable and love the unlovable. You will discover the secret of Louada's life, which is hidden in the cross of Jesus Christ.

I have never known anyone who lived through such abuse as a child and yet has become such an amazing minister for the Lord. Maybe that's why she drips with compassion and love, for when she found Jesus at the age of ten, she took off like a jet plane. She soared off the runway, leaving behind her abusers as she ministered in the presence of God. Then she circled back and led them to the Lord!

She surrendered so totally to the Holy Spirit that He called her into ministry right away. She was only twelve when she received the call of God to preach and teach and minister in music around the world.

This burning call of God on her life has kept her steadily growing in Him. This is what I admire most about her. It is her dogged determination to bring honor to Jesus and to never, never, never give up, in spite of incredible obstacles. This should give us all hope. If Louada could do it, so can we.

In some ways she reminds me of Jesus' mother, Mary, who completely yielded to the will of God for her life. In other ways she reminds me of a female Apostle Paul, who, in spite of the scourgings and imprisonments, the shipwreck and rejections, never let these impediments stop him. *That's Louada!* Though she has experienced a painful childhood and profound challenges as an adult, she has been unstoppable.

As you turn these pages, get ready now to have your hope and vision and purpose restored while reading this heartwarming story of—*Louada!*

ENDNOTE

1 Sandy Davis Kirk, *UNDONE by a Revelation of the Lamb* (Lake Mary, FL: Creation House, 2013).

My Story

A Stunning Triumph of Hope

by Louada Raschke

My heart overflows as I tell you my story. Though filled with heartache and pain, this story bursts with overcoming victory.

I don't tell you my story for my own sake; I don't talk about it so that I can vent. *God forbid!* I write about it because someone like you might need to read it. I want you to know that the same God who set me free can set you free as well. And the same God who set me free can set the abuser free, too. That man or woman who abuses children, a pedophile or rapist, is trapped just like the one being abused.

You may be imprisoned in a situation from which it seems impossible to escape, but we serve a God of the impossible. I don't know what you are going through, or what has ensnared you, but the Holy Spirit knows.

If you carry around a burden of fear or rejection,

please do *not give up*. If you are trying to self-medicate your pain, God wants to heal you completely. I lived in a world of incest and violence and alcoholism and abuse, but God has set me free and given me a ministry beyond my highest dreams. He did it for me—a broken, poverty-stricken, sexually abused little girl—and I know He can do it for you.

Now, before you turn the page and plunge right into the harrowing scene with my drunk momma on the highway, let me explain: I love my momma with all my heart, and her story in itself is an amazing tribute to God's grace. But I want you to know that before she went home to be with Jesus in 2012, she gave me permission to tell her story—our story—with all its painful details. She wanted to encourage *you* with this *stunning triumph of hope.*

1

One Terrifying Night
When I cried out—"Father!"

In a drunken stupor, my momma weaved the car down the dark highway, swerving wildly around onrushing traffic. I was only nine, so I didn't fully realize the danger we were in.

I rested my head on my momma's lap, always glad to be near her. But the moment I started to drift off to sleep, I suddenly heard a deep masculine voice from the back seat of the car: "Get up! Get up NOW!"

With a sudden start, I shot up and turned to look, but no one was there. I looked back over at my momma. Her eyes had rolled back in her head. Her mouth foamed. She had passed out and her head hung outside the open window.

I was frantic. White froth bubbled out of her mouth, dribbling down her chin and blowing away in the wind. To me it looked like my momma had suddenly turned into a monster.

Now the car veered all over the road. I didn't know what to do. I could hear cars honking as they whizzed around her. I screamed out with all my might, *"FATHER!"*

Who was I calling on? Was I shrieking for my own father, whom I had never met? Was I yelling for a make-believe daddy to whom I had written many love notes, wishing I could meet him, longing to know what he looked like and where I could find him? Or was I calling out to the heavenly Father, a God who also seemed illusive, remote, and far away?

I didn't know, but somehow it seemed that whoever it was, he had heard me and sent help. Maybe it really was God? Maybe He had heard my desperate cry and sent an angel to ride with me in the back seat of our car.

Only God knew how dreadfully chaotic my life had become. Since I was six years old, Momma started drinking. She began with Vodka in the morning, then chased it with straight whiskey, then another Vodka and whiskey all day long until she finally passed out at night.

She was trying to medicate her horrific pain from the physical and emotional scars that tore at her soul. I tried to take care of her, but I couldn't. I was only a little girl who loved and adored my momma. I knew she adored me too, but she couldn't help herself. She was drowning in her own sea of pain and alcoholism.

Along with the drinking, she tried to numb her pain by sleeping with many men, but what she didn't realize is what those men were doing to me. She was always too drunk to know that those men were sexually violating me as well.

I was a broken little girl, full of fear and insecurity. I was being passed around from man to man and home to home. Starting from the age of six my own uncle abused me regularly, and he was a big man, really big. He was violent; he was a drunk; and he even used a knife sometimes to threaten me.

Whenever he finished using me, he gave me money. I didn't know what to do with that money. It seemed like dirty money to me. So I hid it inside one of my dolls, in the place where batteries are held. Nobody knew.

Now, here I was, a frightened little girl, in a runaway car, careening uncontrollably down the highway. Somehow, I must rise up and take charge of a situation that was headed for certain tragedy.

I didn't know anything about how to drive a car, but I had cried out from the depths of my being, "Father," and He was helping me. I grabbed the steering wheel and with cars coming straight toward me, I veered in and out of traffic, dodging the oncoming cars.

My mother had twisted her body and was slumping down, causing her foot to press even harder on the accelerator. I didn't know a gas pedal from a brake pedal, but I somehow pulled my momma's leg off the gas and reached my leg over to push on the brakes, all the while steering around the onrushing traffic. The car slowed down, and I maneuvered it over to the shoulder of the road, gradually bringing it to a stop.

I don't know how I knew to do it, but I guess it was an angel helping me. I shifted the car into park, turned off the power, and jumped out of the car.

In absolute panic, I ran out in the middle of the highway, screaming, "Help me! Help me! My mother has turned into a monster!" Cars swerved around me, not bothering to help this skinny little nine-year-old girl. I was petrified.

Finally, an older couple saw me and turned around. "Honey, can we help you?" they asked kindly.

I cried, "Something's happened to my momma. I don't know what it is. She's turned into a monster. I don't know what to do!"

These sweet people helped me and my mother to safety, but from that moment on I was a terrorized little girl. I felt afraid of all the men who were abusing me. I feared my own mother, yet I couldn't bear to be separated from her. I loved her with all my heart, and no one could ever take away my love for her or her love for me. Now, in the next chapter, I want to tell you a little more about my broken momma.

~

First, however, let me forewarn you. As you read my story, there may be times you feel like putting your head down to cry. *Please do.* Getting grief out is vital to your own full healing. But don't cry for me. Don't cry in self-pity. Cry because you feel Jesus touching the pain in your own heart. He wants you to weep those tears of grief out on His nail-scarred feet.

So, before I continue with my story, let me ask—what about you? Have you been filled with fears like mine? Have you been sexually abused and too afraid to tell anyone? Has your life been threatened if you dared to expose the abuser? Are you trapped in an inescapable situation?

If so, I can't wait to tell you what God did for me. You may not even believe in God. You may feel hurt with Him because of something painful in your life, and you may be blaming Him.

If you are carrying around a feeling of hurt and rejection. . . of anger or regret. . . I promise you this—God loves you and He wants to heal your wounded heart.

If you need the Lord to heal your pain from abuse, or if someone you love needs to be free of drugs, alcohol, or sexual abuse, please keep reading.

As I tell you my story, I will be completely vulnerable and raw with you. I will tell you the good, the bad, and the ugly.

It may hurt to read such a shocking story because there were times I felt like I couldn't keep going. I wanted to give up, but the Lord always seemed to break through to help me. He would give me the faith and the hope to *never, never give up!* I know He will do this for you, too.

Let me now open up my heart and tell you more about my momma. And please remember that, before my momma went to be with Jesus in 2012, she gave me her permission to tell our story (see Preface). It's a sad story but it will eventually lead to a very happy ending. . .

2

My Broken Momma
A Child's Unconditional Love

No one knew the hell I was experiencing behind closed doors. Incest, violence, divorce, fighting that sometimes erupted into knives and stabbing and even guns. I often saw my momma bloodied and bruised from some man beating her up.

I loved my momma so much. When I was young, I didn't understand why she had all those men and why she stayed drunk so much. But one thing I did know—my momma loved me.

In fact, she adored me, and I can tell you that I adored her, too. With all the love a little girl could ever hold in her heart, I loved her unconditionally.

Through my tears, I could see her drunken state and all I wanted to do was help her and make her feel better. Her life was so busted and unhappy.

As I got older, I saw even more how shattered she really was. But it never made me love her any less. It made me want to protect and care for her even more.

Though a mother can wound her child with her destructive lifestyle, she can never destroy her love.

Actually, in many ways, I mothered her. I realize now that no little girl should have to shoulder such a heavy burden. But to me, at the time, I was glad to do it. Why? Because I loved my broken momma.

At times, I lived in a car with Momma, other times with aunts and uncles and grandparents. Momma never had a home unless she had a man to provide it. By then she had been married five times, and in the midst of it all, I had been abused terribly. I had begun to turn inward, becoming a shy, fearful, timid child. No one knew what was happening to me.

But through it all, I knew my momma loved me. She would do anything she could for me, but she simply didn't know how to take care of me. Most of the time, we hardly had enough money for food. She would feed me a little can of potted meat or Vienna sausages or maybe a sandwich from a convenience store, and I was happy to have it. Of course, the real problem was the alcohol addiction, which had taken over her life and completely drained all of our finances.

Most people didn't know this, but my momma could sing. Before she started drinking, she loved going to church where pastors usually invited her to sing a solo.

Once she was even invited to sing in one of the great A.A. Allen's healing meetings. She had a country and western twang that southerners loved. Here she saw genuine miracles before her very eyes.

The Lord blessed me as well with a voice like Momma's. I remember the time in a bar, when she put me up on a table in my little white boots. She gave me the mic and had me sing, "These Boots Are Made for Walkin'." The men loved it and cheered loudly.

I will have to admit that sometimes, when I was feeling really sad about my momma's condition, I would think—*If she really loved me, she would give up her drinking.* But she couldn't. I understood that she was trapped. She couldn't take care of me, much less herself. I felt like it was my job to try to take care of her. I was only nine, but I still tried.

Like I said, much of the time, we lived in our car, and she would gamble at casinos, trying to make a little money. When she was really drunk, I would always make sure she made it safely to the car. If she was too drunk to eat, I would try to get her to eat something. If she was too drunk to drive, I would hide the keys. I had learned a lesson the hard way about Momma and drunk driving.

I would sometimes hide her billfold so she wouldn't be able to buy alcohol. She just couldn't help herself. She would have given her life for me. She thought I walked on water, but she didn't know how to care for me and keep me safe.

I remember one Christmas, when we had no money, Momma went out and sold some of her possessions. She went searching for presents for me and my half-brother. She came home with a little parakeet and a Chihuahua dog. We were thrilled. That day we even had Christmas dinner at Weiner Schnitzel!

Momma worked part-time as a bartender, but we were on the go a lot, too. Sometimes she would get so bad, she couldn't work. She couldn't get food. She was out of control and passing out frequently. And her driving would become impossible. She got so many DWIs that there was a warrant out for her arrest. She was always running from the Law.

Often, I would have to call Grandma and Grandpa, her parents, and ask them to come get her and put her in a rehab. That's when I would have to go live with them, and it was miserable.

She couldn't drive to come see me because of all the DWIs, but sometimes she would slip out late at night to my grandparents' home and tiptoe into their trailer to spend a few hours with me. She always loved me, no matter what, and I loved my momma.

She finally came to a point she had to be admitted to the huge mental health drug and alcohol rehab center in Big Spring, Texas. She had wine sores all over her body. Her skin was yellow, and she was told that she must stop drinking, or she would die.

My grandparents told her that she absolutely could not have me living with her anymore. This caused her to sink even lower. Momma cried and pleaded for her baby girl, but they concluded that it was too dangerous for me. I cried my heart out over this. I just wanted to be with my momma.

～

I hope and pray you have not had to go through this kind of heartache. But maybe you have. Keep on reading my story because it is about to make a marvelous turn. What I am about to tell you will change your whole life if you will allow it.

Do you remember when I told you about the time when Momma was driving drunk and out of control, and I cried out with all my might, *"Father!"* That was the beginning of the miracle.

I felt like, if I only had a father—a real father—to protect me from all the abusive men and now from my grandparents' harshness, I could be happy. Little did I know what was about to happen in less than a year.

Now, let me tell you how, in the midst of my sorrow and shame, a father really did reach out to help me. This led to the miracle that would change my life forever. It would give me the strength to *never, never give up!*

I know it can happen for you, too. . .

3

A Little Girl Finds a Dad
The Day that Changed My Life

I sat in school with my head always down, fearful that if I made eye contact with the teacher, she or he would call on me.

I was ten years old now, in the fifth grade, and much too full of shame to open my mouth and speak. I felt that nothing I could say would be worth anything. I had no value. Men treated me like a rag doll, simply existing for their own pleasure.

One day in class, while lost in my thoughts, I heard my name being called over the loudspeaker: "Louada Harrison, please come to the office."

All eyes turned toward me. My face blushed and my heart raced. *Oh no! What have I done? Did I make a mistake? Why would I be called to the office?* In my mind, only bad people were called to the principal's office.

The teacher motioned for me to go, and I slowly walked down the long corridor, sick with fear. As I entered the glass door, I saw a strange man sitting with the principal. He stood and smiled awkwardly at me.

I could feel the beads of sweat slipping down my face and neck. I thought my heart would pound right out of my chest. The principal said warmly, "Louada, I would like to introduce you to your father."

What? I thought. *This man is my own father? This is the one I had secretly written love notes to, never knowing where to send them? This is the one I would dream of meeting someday, even telling him I missed him so much, though I had never even met him?*

"Really?" I mumbled, half in shock.

I just looked at him and stared, too stunned to speak. He had an olive complexion, dark hair streaked with flecks of silver, and cool blue eyes. We didn't hug or shake hands. He, too, seemed to be at a loss for words.

We made a little small talk, and then he told me he wanted to bring his wife and come visit me. Because I was living with my grandparents, we had to get their permission first. They cautiously agreed, and my dad, Bill Harrison and his wife, came to see me.

At my grandparents' trailer, we met again. His kind demeanor and gentle spirit began to melt my defenses toward him. He had brought his wife, and now they were telling me about my three half-sisters and a half-brother. I couldn't wait to meet my new family.

Eventually, Grandma and Grandpa agreed to allow me to visit them at their home. I soon discovered that my dad had quit drinking and had become a Christian. Then something happened that I will never ever forget.

In gentle tones, he said, "Emma Lou," (that was my birth name) "I know I let you down as a father, but I want to tell you about a Father who will never let you down. I want to tell you about a God who loves you and sent His only Son to save you from all the pain and heartache you have experienced."

He paused, as his words soaked in.

What? I thought. In all my life, I had never heard such beautiful words. I looked at him in silence, but my eyes conveyed to him that I was open and hungry. I desperately wanted to hear more!

I leaned forward, trying to blink back my tears. But I couldn't hold them back. Tears of hope washed shamelessly down my face.

Bill had a little Bible with him, and he gave it to me. "This is for you," he said, but first he opened it to John 3:16 and read, "'For God so loved the world,'—that means God so loved you, Emma Lou—'that He gave His only begotten Son, that whoever believes in Him shall not perish, but have eternal life.'"

I had never even read the Bible, but now my dad was telling me that Jesus Christ, God's only Son, came down to earth for the primary purpose of laying down His life. He took all my sins to the cross where He was crucified for me.

"Not only your sin, Emma Lou, but all those in your life who have hurt you." At that point, my dad had no idea about the brutal men who abused me. He didn't even know about my momma's drinking. But then he said, "Jesus took all my sin for abandoning you and leaving you without a dad."

I could hardly contain my emotion. If he only knew what it had been like to grow up without the protection of a real father. I drank in his words like a thirsty child in the midst of a hot burning desert.

"And that's not all," he whispered, with tears now filling his eyes and dripping down his cheeks. It was like every word he spoke was dipped in God's love. He went on, "Then God poured down punishment on His innocent Son. Jesus was punished in your place, in the place of anyone who has ever hurt you."

"But why?" I asked.

"Because He loves you and He wants to save you!" I thought of my family, which was drenched in sin. I pictured the chaos, the yelling and cussing, the knives and guns, the trampling of God's name, and the absolute bedlam.

"You see, Emma Lou, Jesus died but He rose again. After three days He came out of the tomb and then He ascended into heaven, and now He wants to come to you and save you and make you His child."

Those words blew my heart wide open. But now it was time for me to get home, so Bill and his wife Gail drove me to my grandparents' trailer. Before I got out of the car, he asked if he could take me to church next Sunday. I was ecstatic! When Grandma and Grandpa saw my excitement, they nodded. I could hardly wait for Sunday to come.

I counted the days, even the hours, until Sunday morning dawned. Rising early, I searched for my best clothes to wear. All my clothes came from thrift stores, but I did the best I could to dress up for church. I knew something wonderful was going to happen to me, and I wanted to be dressed for the occasion.

Bill and Gail drove me to a little Baptist church in Lubbock. When I walked in, I noticed the atmosphere felt good. The church was filled with gentle-hearted, loving people who made me feel right at home.

I sat down by my dad and looked to the front of the church. Hanging on the wall was a rugged-looking cross. It held my gaze as I thought of all the things my dad had told me about Jesus dying on the cross.

What struck me most was that Jesus loved me, little me, a lonely, forgotten, neglected little girl. But He loved me and died to save me. I didn't fully understand what that meant, but I wanted it with all my heart.

All through the sermon, my eyes stayed rivetted on that cross. I kept wondering—would Jesus really save me? The preacher concluded his message with an altar call for all who wanted to give their lives to Christ.

My dad looked over at me and gently asked, "Would you like to go forward? I'll go with you if you want to give your life to Jesus."

I nodded enthusiastically, and together we walked to the altar. I clutched my little Bible as we knelt down. Already the tears were flowing. My dad reached over to open my Bible. He showed me the verse, "If we confess our sins, He is faithful and righteous to forgive us our sins and to cleanse us from all unrighteousness" (1 John 1:9).

He led me in the sinner's prayer, and I sincerely confessed my sins, telling the Lord how sorry I was. Now the tears were spilling shamelessly down my face and wetting the collar of my dress. It was sincere repentance from the heart of a desperate little girl.

Then Dad turned to a verse in Revelation 3:20: "Behold I stand at the door and knock. If anyone hears

My voice and opens the door, I will come in. . ." He whispered, "Jesus is knocking. Now open wide your heart and let Him come in."

He led me in a prayer to open my heart and ask Jesus Christ to come inside and live His life in me. And do you know what happened? He did! Jesus Christ, the Son of God, came into my heart and I embraced him with my whole being. I was His and He was mine. I knew it! I absolutely knew that I was SAVED!

What's more, it was my own dad who led me to Him. To be honest, we never really had what I would call a close relationship, but I will never ever forget that he is the one God used to bring me into this world and to lead me to the Lord. He was promoted to heaven in January of 2022, and I am eternally grateful for how God used him in my life.

That day I went home to my grandparents now with a joy and a peace like I had never known in my life. I can't say that my circumstances changed. My grandparents still worked me like a slave, and I was still being abused by family members. But I had JESUS!

I read in my Bible that I had been born again (John 3:7). And that's exactly how I felt. I felt like a brand-new person. I had peace and hope and I had a father—a Heavenly Father—who loved me and cared for me.

At last, a little girl had found a Father—a real Father, who had always loved me and would never forsake me. It was the answer to my desperate cry, which I had screamed out in that runaway car—*"Father!"*

From that day on, I tried to walk with God every single day. I prayed about everything. I prayed when I took tests. I prayed about how to spell certain words.

I entered spelling contests, and guess what? I won first place in the Spelling Bee! Best of all, Jesus was my best friend, and I knew I would never be alone again. And yet, little did I know that He had so much more in store for me. He would give me an encounter with the Holy Spirit and call me into ministry.

~

But before I tell you what happened next, which was even more than I could have ever imagined, I want to ask you—have you prayed to receive Jesus Christ as your Savior? Before you close these pages, please turn back and read again about my repentance for sin and then pray to ask Him into your heart.

Remember, Jesus is knocking, and He wants to come inside you. Even in the midst of the sorrow and pain of your life, He wants to save you and be your very best friend. He wants to be the Father you may never have known.

Ask Him now to come. . . Whisper, "Come, Lord Jesus." He will come into your heart and change everything. But then, He will do even more. I can hardly wait to tell you about it. He will put a fire in your heart, like He did in mine, and it will encourage you to *never, never give up!*

4

Baptized in the Holy Spirit
Overflowing in My Prayer Language

My grandparents loved me, and I loved them, but they worked me like a grown man. They owned a trailer park, and every day I had to carry heavy barrels of trash, clean out filthy trailers, and mow the grass.

The work was grueling for an eleven-year-old little girl. The hardest part of all was the ache I felt in my heart for my momma.

Maybe I should have been glad when my dad and Gail wanted to get custody of me. They filed a court case and fought hard to take me away from Grandma and Grandpa.

I felt torn because I knew if I went with my dad, I would never get to see my momma. At least sometimes she could slip away and come visit me at my grandparents' trailer.

Finally, the judge asked me who I wanted to live with. I told him I wanted to stay with my grandparents, but I didn't tell him why. The truth was that I wanted to be near my momma.

Now, because of the court case, Grandma and Grandpa did not want me going to church anymore with my dad. They moved us to another town, Vernon, Texas, so I wouldn't be around him.

Now they started dropping me off at a little Assemblies of God church. I was thankful to be in church, and this turned out to be an amazing blessing.

I went by myself and sat alone, feeling nervous, scared and out of place. But then something wonderful happened. A warm-hearted older lady named Mrs. Pennington came up to me. I think she sensed how lonely I felt. "How old are you, Honey?" she asked.

"I'm eleven," I said shyly.

"Well, today, you will be twelve! I want you to come be part of my Sunday School class which is filled with students twelve and older." She even promised to pick me up at the trailer park, take me to church, and bring me home.

Ruth Pennington was a great teacher. She was anointed, and while the other teenagers played around in class, I hung on every word. She taught us about the doctrine of the Assemblies of God, but most of all she talked about Jesus and about being filled with the Holy Spirit. She poured her life into me, and she had a profound impact during a critical time of my life. I will never forget her.

Then came the week-long revival. Brother and Sister Metzger were the evangelists, and they were amazing. All week long the teenagers were encouraged to be seeking the Holy Spirit. I was so hungry. I began praying earnestly, night and day, that I could be filled—or as they said, BAPTIZED—in the Holy Spirit.

They explained that the Holy Spirit came inside us when we were saved. But now He wanted to immerse us, baptize us, with the Spirit. They told us they were going to lay their hands on us, like Jesus said to do, and the Holy Spirit would come upon us in power.

They said if we would surrender our voices and tongues to Him, He would pray through us in another language. It sounded exciting, but I wondered if this could really happen for me.

Thursday night was the big night. Brother Metzger called the teenagers to come to the front and make a line. My body began to tremble as they prayed for each young person, and as they came closer and closer to me, I shook even more.

Finally, they came to me. They both laid their hands on me and simply said, "Be filled NOW, and just begin speaking the words out of your mouth."

BAM! The Holy Spirit hit me like a bolt of lightning. I fell to the floor bursting out in tongues and praying fluently for 45 minutes in my prayer language. I could have laid there praying all night, but they began turning off the lights and trying to clear the church.

I also knew that Mrs. Pennington was waiting on me. But I was so drunk in the spirit that she had to help me to the car.

That night I went to sleep with a peace like I had never known in all my life. I felt like I was floating on a cloud of God's presence. I don't remember my dreams, but I know they were full of peace and love.

And though the circumstances around me would remain the same with family members involved in incest, violence, fighting, stabbing, drinking, and cursing, it didn't matter. I had a peace and a power inside that would carry me through the roughest times. There were still many painful roads ahead, but I cannot wait to tell you about the new boldness that filled me. I shocked myself at the way I was now able to stand up to my abusers. You will love hearing this part of my story.

~

Now I must ask you. Are you hungry for the Holy Spirit? Do you want to receive all God has for you? All I know is, I needed more of God, and I suspect you do to. Life is tough, and if you are reading this book, you have probably experienced some of the pain I've been telling you about.

I can only tell you this—the Holy Spirit is the power of God, but He is also as gentle as a dove. He is one of the three Persons in the Godhead, and He will be beautifully personal with you. He will lead you with the sweet fire of His presence. And when you need His boldness to stand up for truth, He will empower you like He did me.

So if you desire for Him to baptize you and flow through you with the evidence of speaking in tongues, ask Him now. Be sure your heart is clean, especially from any new age or occult practices. If you have dabbled in any of this, ask Him to forgive you and wash you clean in the blood of the Lamb.

Now, like a little child, open wide and ask the Holy Spirit to COME . . . Whisper, "Come, Holy Spirit... Come and fill me now." Reach up and receive Him deeply into your spirit. Let His gentle rushing wind fill you. Breathe Him in deeply. Drink your fill of His wonderful goodness and glory.

And now, with childlike faith, open your mouth and begin to speak. With His presence flooding down upon you, give Him your voice, your tongue, your vocal cords, and pray to Him in your prayer language. Let it flow. . . and flow. . . and flow. This language will become very important to you in the days to come.

In fact, even now, go to your Bible and read 1 Corinthians 14. Notice how Paul thanks God that he speaks in tongues more than all them (1 Cor. 14:18). He says he will pray in the spirit and pray in his known language. He will sing in the spirit and sing in his known language (1 Cor. 14:15).

He says that the purpose of praying in the spirit, which means praying in tongues, is to speak mysteries to God (1 Cor. 14:2). It will edify you (1 Cor. 14:4), which means to build you up spiritually. Praying in tongues is such a blessing, and it is your own private language between you and God (1 Cor. 14:2a).

Furthermore, read what happened when the Holy Spirit came down in Acts 2:1-13, Acts 8:14-17, Acts 10:44-46, and Acts 19:1-6. I promise you—the blessed baptism in the Holy Spirit will change your life completely.

And now, when you go to bed tonight, you can lay your head on your pillow with a sense of overwhelming peace. Though circumstances around you may not have changed, *you* have changed. Now you have the Comforter himself living inside you and flowing out of you. He will help you understand the Bible and He will bring you closer and closer to Jesus.

Wait till you hear about the incredible new boldness He gave me to stand up to my abusers. I think you will be as amazed as I was. And I believe He will give you this boldness, too. This holy boldness will inspire you to *never, never give up!*

5

Bold as a Lion
Following the Holy Spirit and Fire

I wandered into the kitchen the next day and found Grandma, Grandpa, and Uncle Jack, my sexual abuser, sitting around the table. When I saw that 250-pound, 6'4" man, I went straight to my room and grabbed my doll. I emptied out all the dirty money he had given me through the years.

I stomped into that kitchen as bold as a lion. I threw that guilt money at Jack, pointed my finger in his face, and roared, "You will NEVER touch me again!"

I'm telling you, the fear of God came all over that man. His eyes nearly bugged out of his head. He got up and left as fast as he could, and he never touched me again. Not only did he never touch me improperly but neither did any other man!

God had baptized me in the Holy Spirit and fire, and I was blazing with boldness. It was just like John the Baptist said: "He will baptize you with the Holy Spirit and fire" (Luke 3:16).

I went back to church that night and I felt like a new woman inside. As I said, I was only twelve years old, but because I had stood for truth and purity, the Holy Spirit had given me a new boldness that I never dreamed I could have. It reminded me of the time in Acts 4:31 when "they were all filled with the Holy Spirit and began to speak the word of God with boldness."

At the service that night, I felt the Lord moving on me to ask the pastor if I could sing a Christian song called, "One Day at a Time." Truthfully, I felt terribly afraid to do it, but boldness doesn't mean there is no fear; it means that we overcome fear by doing what the Holy Spirit is telling us, regardless of how we feel.

I had a supernatural, overwhelming desire to serve the Lord. I desperately wanted to be used by Him, so I pushed through my old shyness and stood to sing. My whole body shook so hard I had to hold onto the pulpit in order to stand. It was partly the fear, but even more, it was the power of the Holy Spirit moving upon me.

I later learned that the Holy Spirit trembled over the waters at creation in Genesis 1:2, and He still trembles over His people when He is moving upon them. So I stood before that congregation and sang my little heart out.

It's what the Holy Spirit did next that shocked me. As I sang, shaking like a leaf in a windstorm, the power of

God fell. People began streaming to the altar, weeping, crying out to God, praying in the spirit, kneeling, and some were even falling under the power of the Spirit.

The pastor asked me to keep on singing that one song, and the people kept responding. I knew it was not me for sure. It was all Him. I was amazed at what He was doing in the people when He came on them.

They were overcome with love for God. Some of them repented of sin while others rejoiced in the presence of the Lord. Some of them were healed and others simply bowed in humble gratitude. That night I was forever ruined for the true power of God's Spirit. I knew I could do nothing without Him.

Finally, I stopped singing and began laying hands on people. I began prophesying and giving words of knowledge, which I had never done in all my life. The Bible talks about these gifts which help to heal and encourage others, but remember, I was only twelve years old, and this was all so new for me.

It was here at church that I found my voice. Before that, I was shy and withdrawn and easily intimidated. I never spoke out or expressed myself. I was as mute as a mouse; now I was bold as a lion. By that I mean I was bold when the Spirit of God was upon me. I was like a different person. I had found a wonderful new courage and I knew it came from the Holy Spirit.

At some point during the night, the Holy Spirit spoke to me personally. His stunning words have stayed with me forever. He said, "I have called you to preach and teach and minister in music all over the world!"

Really? Me? It was beyond my wildest dream, but with that word He also gave me the faith to believe it could someday happen.

During this critical time of my early Christian life, the Lord sent me two mentors, Ruth Pennington and Marvis Gabriel. Marvis was like a spiritual mother to me, and she didn't hesitate to bring me "spiritual spankings" whenever I needed it. Once her daughter, Donna James, asked, "Mom, why are you so hard on Louada?"

She said, "Because of the call of God on her life!" I will always be grateful to Marvis for affirming my calling and helping me grow in Christ. Whenever I felt a little down, she would remind me, "Lord, keep me when I don't want to be kept; and hold me when I don't want to be held."

Now I began to sing in the choir and sing solos in church. I even began to step out in leadership. In the next few years, I became a Children's Church leader. I spoke at Missionette meetings. And I became president of Youth Alive at my high school.

Can you believe it? The little girl who kept her head down at school and never wanted to speak a word because she felt so fearful and worthless now had found her voice. Most of all, she had received a call from God. I know He can do this for you, too.

~

I'm not saying you will become a preacher. Yes, that's my calling, but you may be called to minister mercy to others. You may be called to offer help to people in need. God may call you to teach or to write or to sing and compose songs. He may give you a gift of leadership and of speaking.

You may have a special love for little children, with a yearning to minister to them and lead them closer to Jesus. You may be a great organizer and administrator. You may be an amazing people person, gathering people together for ministry to the Lord. You may be brilliant at making money, and God can use you to help fund ministries. The list is endless, but here is the key—*seek the Holy Spirit.*

Let Him fill you, and when He gives you a special burden or moves upon you to do something for Him, do it. That's what He did for me when He first moved me to sing that song in church. So here is what I am really saying—*follow the fire.*

When the Holy Spirit is on something, follow what He shows you. Keep on following the movings of the Holy Spirit until you discover your call from God. He will call you into the very thing you do best. He will sharpen your gifting and use you for His glory. Though you may have once felt worthless and without value or purpose in life, you will find your worth in Him.

Now I must tell you about another sad time in my life, but I also have something wonderful to tell you as well. In the beginning of this book, I told you that I would be raw and vulnerable as I tell you my story. I said I would tell you the good, the bad, and the ugly. This time, I will tell you about a time that I actually did give up, but the Lord saved me just in time.

I want to be painfully real with you now, but first I can hardly wait to tell you something fabulous that happened to my precious momma. . .

6

My Hidden Shame and Pain

Washed in the Blood of the Lamb

My momma quit drinking!

I could just cry telling you this now. When the doctor told her she would die if she ever drank again, she got serious about it. She didn't want to leave me motherless, and she knew she wasn't ready to face God.

You must wonder how, after all these years of addiction, she could quit. It was God! She cried out to Him with all her heart, and He heard her prayer. He delivered her completely, and though she had to go through some difficult days of withdrawal, the Holy Spirit carried her through. It was a genuine miracle.

I was worried sick, however, when I heard she had gotten a job again as a bartender. But that was all she knew how to do to earn money, and she never touched another drop of alcohol.

One day a handsome young man in his late thirties sauntered into the bar. He ordered a drink, took one look at my beautiful momma, and fell in love. Interestingly, they were both backslidden from the Assemblies of God church. Jack Turner was soon to retire from the Air Force, and he would then be offered a high-powered job in Saudi Arabia. He began dating my mom, but when he asked her to marry him, she said, "No. I will never marry any man who drinks!"

That was all it took. He, too, quit drinking and they were joyously wed. This was momma's sixth husband, but it was a marriage made in heaven. They were both deliriously in love and it made me so happy.

I look back now, and I realize that God used "Daddy" to save our whole family. I have always called him Daddy because he loves me and my momma so much, and he is such a wonderful Christian man. He has always been so good to both of us. In fact, I have to tell you, Daddy is by far the greatest man I have ever known. He is a beautiful example of our heavenly Father.

All this time, he and Momma were giving money to my grandparents to care for my needs. They even gave them extra so I would have a little spending money, but to be honest, I hardly ever saw any of it.

I loved my grandparents and they loved me, but they were very cruel to me, especially Grandpa. As I told you earlier, they treated me like a slave, lifting heavy barrels and cleaning dirty trailers. I also had to mow the lawn at the trailer park, even in the blazing heat of the day. One day, Grandpa, just to prove his dominance and control over me, forced me to cut the grass, in the burning hot sun, with a pair of scissors!

Momma couldn't bear to see my suffering. She and Daddy arranged to rent an apartment for me so I could get away from this slave labor. Daddy was soon to leave for Saudi Arabia, and I assumed Momma would be living with me in the apartment.

I was ecstatic with happiness. At last, after the horrible years of drunkenness and abusive male visitors, I would get to be with my momma. She was sober now, and I could get to know my real momma. We would cook together, eat meals together, sleep in the same apartment, and shop together like moms and daughters, and best of all—go to church together. I could hardly wait!

I wondered what was going on one day when I found that Daddy ordered two plane tickets to Saudi Arabia. I thought, *Is Momma going to leave me?*

Then the bomb dropped and shattered my soul into a million pieces. She said, "Baby, Daddy has to get back to work, so we will be leaving to go back to Saudi Arabia. But we wanted to be sure you had a nice place to live."

Her words struck me with a heavy thud. It felt like a

hole blew open in the bottom of my soul and my heart fell right through it.

"But . . . but I thought . . ." I didn't finish the sentence because I didn't want her to know how devastated I was. I honestly thought she had gotten us the apartment so we could live together my senior year. I was seventeen and soon to graduate, but I still needed my momma. The thought of living alone terrified me and made me feel rejected and depressed.

I tried hard to hide my feelings. I forced a smile and said I understood. I pushed my hurt down and never exposed it until many years later.

I know I had Jesus and was filled with the Holy Spirit and that God had called me to serve Him. But I couldn't handle the pain. Depression overtook me and I lost my desire to live.

One day, I got so depressed that I gave up. I swallowed a bottle of Midol pills. I didn't really want to die, but I couldn't bear to live. Looking back now, I realize it was a cry for help.

Just before I passed out, I called my pastor and told him what I had done. He rushed me to the ER where my stomach was pumped. Then he called my parents in Saudi Arabia and told them they needed to come home and help me. As soon as he could, Daddy quit his job and he and momma began the process of moving back to Texas.

Meanwhile, in my deep loneliness, I started looking for love in all the wrong places. I dropped out of school and couldn't even bring myself to go to church anymore. I think I must have been hurt with God for leaving me all alone without a mother.

Even though my life was filled with chaos before, at least I had never lived alone. I found a nice boy named Donnie. He had a good job and we moved in together, which of course meant we were sleeping together before marriage.

I was so convicted that I could hardly bear it. I was a Christian and I knew this was wrong, but Donnie didn't seem too interested in marriage.

When my parents finally got back, they bought a house in Kerrville, Texas and planned to move me in with them. They moved me out of the apartment and as we were driving to the new house, suddenly a bright yellow Dodge Charger sped up beside us, honking loudly.

It was Donnie. When he realized that I had left him and was going with my parents, he suddenly had a change of heart. He motioned for us to pull over to the shoulder of the road. Then he jumped out and I met him beside the road. He begged me not to leave him and asked if I would marry him.

I was still a teenager, but I said, "Yes," and in three days, we were married. I loved him with all my heart, but soon conviction struck me. I thought to myself, *What have I done?*

I realized I was no longer pressing into God, no longer turning to Him and presenting my pain and wounds to Him for healing, no longer reading my Bible or going to church. I also felt bad that I had hurt Grandma and Grandpa, and most of all I felt guilty and condemned for the sexual sin before marriage.

Yet, through it all, I could still hear the Lord's voice ringing in my spirit, reminding me of my calling: "I have called you to preach and teach and minister in music throughout the world."

At last, I knew what I must do. I headed straight for church. I fell at the altar and sobbed out my repentance. The Lord gave me a gift of repentance, and godly grief swept over me. I confessed my sins and named them one by one. Then I reached out to the cross and let the blood of Jesus Christ wash me clean.

Oh, thank God for the power of the blood of the Lamb! Jesus forgave me and washed me and cleansed me and took away all my guilt and shame. Thank God He promises, "If we confess our sins, He is faithful and righteous to forgive us our sins and to cleanse us from all unrighteousness," for indeed "the blood of Jesus His Son cleanses us from all sin" (1 John 1:9, 7).

I'm telling you, when I finally got up from that altar, I looked a mess, but I was no longer a mess inside. I was washed, I was cleansed, I was purged, I was delivered, and I was fully forgiven by God.

~

I hope you have never backslidden away from God like I did, but if you have, can I give you the solution? Run back to the cross!

Come to the place where the blood of the Lamb flows like a crimson tide. Ask Him to give you a gift of repentance and turn completely from your sin. He will wash you and cleanse you and take away all your guilt and shame. Oh, thank God for the blood of the Lamb!

Now my heart began to come alive again. I started ministering to people and preaching and singing, just like before. I knew that I was forgiven, and this time, I knew—I would *never, never give up again!*

Now, I am excited to tell you what happened next. Though I knew I was forgiven, I still had so many people in my life I needed to forgive. . .

7

Forgiving the Unforgivable
The Grace to Let Go of Bitterness

One day, Bill and I were sitting in his living room as he drank his coffee and I sipped my tea. I opened up my heart and tried to be vulnerable with him. These were questions I had carried for years.

"Dad, why did you and Momma abandon me and reject me and put me in harm's way? You left me open to the abuse of men, and it hurt so badly. Many many men forced me to perform sex acts on them, and it made me feel so ashamed. I felt like damaged goods."

I was letting out feelings that I had never even told my momma because I knew she couldn't handle it. I was finally having an honest talk with this man who deserted me and left me so vulnerable to abuse. It felt good to get out these buried emotions.

The blood rose to my face and stained my cheeks. I continued, "I couldn't understand why you left me, and why you never wanted to see me. How could you discard your little girl?"

Bill could only hang his head in regret. Finally, he muttered, "I'm so sorry I wasn't in your life. The Lord has broken my heart over it. I started a bus ministry for children, hoping that if I reached out to kids, someone would reach out to you."

Bill remained calm and soft-spoken. "Emma Lou, won't you please, please forgive me?"

Suddenly the love of God flooded me. I looked at him with compassion and said, "Yes, Dad, I do forgive. I forgive you with all my heart."

I knew that in that moment, Jesus was giving me the grace to forgive. In fact, He said in the Lord's Prayer that we should forgive others as God has forgiven us. God had forgiven me of so much; how could I hold on to bitterness toward my dad for leaving me?

But not everyone asks forgiveness with such gentle sincerity and humble contrition. He was genuinely sorry. But what about those who are not sorry? Those who feel no guilt or conviction, or at least won't admit it? How do we forgive the unforgivable?

One of the first breakthroughs came when the Holy Spirit gave me the grace to forgive Uncle Jack. Once I stood up to him, not only did I forgive him, but I helped him get right with God. I prayed with him to receive the baptism in the Holy Spirit and the fire of God fell on him.

One day, many years later, I told my story to my

friend, Dr. Sandy. I said, "I have never told anyone about the pain I felt when Momma said she and Daddy were going back to Saudi Arabia."

Dr. Sandy later told me she could feel God's tears in her heart as I told her this story. Then I admitted the suicide attempt, when I took the Midol pills and had to have my stomach pumped. I was ashamed to tell it, but it was somehow a relief to release this pent-up hurt and bring it into the light.

Sandy looked in my eyes and said, "Louada, has anyone ever stood in for your momma and repented to you?"

"No. *No!*" I blurted. It surprised me that she would ask such a question. It seemed like those words drilled right into my heart, unearthing what I had held inside for so long.

Then she said, "May I stand in for your momma and repent to you?"

I quietly gasped. "I-I guess so."

She pulled a chair closer and took my hand. She looked into my eyes and started repenting for all the times I had been left alone, the drunken episodes, for leaving me vulnerable to men, for never having nice food or nice clothes. But most of all, she repented for leaving me and going to Saudi Arabia during my senior year.

"I'm so sorry. I was wrong to hurt you like that," she said, standing in the gap for my momma.

I laid my head over on her shoulder and sobbed. Honestly, of all the painful experiences with my momma, the one that hurt me most was when she was sober at last, and I thought I could finally have a real relationship with her. I had built such a mountain of high hopes, and now the mountain of hope had come tumbling down.

Dr. Sandy waited until all my tears dried, and then she laid her hand on my heart and prayed for the Holy Spirit to wipe away the scar of grief and unforgiveness.

It felt so good to release all that pent-up grief. And I learned a new step of forgiveness. We have to weep out the grief—she calls it "weeping in the river"—before we can fully forgive. I found that releasing grief unlocks forgiveness and forgiveness breaks the chains.

I've already told you how He broke off of me the fear and insecurity. But I didn't realize I had such a fear of being alone. Once I repented for the way I tried to fill my loneliness by sleeping with my future husband, I was able to break that fear of loneliness from my life.

The devil wanted me to fall into the trap of alcoholism like my sweet momma. But God gave me the authority and the power to stand up in the anointing of the Holy Spirit and say, "No, Devil, I will not turn to alcohol to soothe my pain. And I will not turn to sexual sin ever again. I will, from now on, turn to Jesus Christ who *never, never gave up!*"

That's why I continually ask the Lord to keep me near the cross. Even as spikes were driving through Jesus' tender hands and feet, He was forgiving His enemies, even those He loved. He asks us to do the same.

~

Now I must ask you—are you still carrying unforgiveness? What is the most painful experience you have ever had in your life? I know that's a probing question, but you don't want to carry any more grief and anger inside. Not any. You want your heart to be pure "for from it flow the springs of life" (Prov. 4:23).

You may feel like you have already forgiven, maybe a thousand times, but do you still feel any pain or irritation when you think of the person or the incident? If so, let me stand in for the person who hurt you. Whether a mom or dad, a husband, a sibling or friend—let me say to you:

I am so sorry for the hurt this caused you. If I knew your story, I would be more specific, but Jesus knows. So right now, I call you to come kneel at the foot of the cross.

In your own heart, picture Jesus, bleeding and carrying your hurt and shame. Whisper out loud to Him. . . Tell Him all about what happened. Cry at His feet until you can imagine Him wrapping his nail-pierced hands and His aching arms around you. Pour out your tears on Him. No one understands like Jesus. Weep in His arms until the tears are all released.

You see, a wound of the soul is like a physical wound in the flesh. Though it may be covered over with a scab, beneath the crust lays a pulsing lesion filled with infection. Letting tears of grief pour out on Jesus is the first step in healing the wounds of your heart.

Once you have wept out your grief, look up again at your beautiful Jesus. . . Gaze into His eyes of love. . . Lock eyes with Him and let His Calvary Love flow into your heart. . . Deeply, purely, richly. . . Drink in His amazing love.

And when you are ready, ask Him to fill you afresh with His resurrection power. This is the power of the Holy Spirit, but let Him come. . . Let His divine nature pour into your heart, healing, renewing, filling you with more of himself. He will give you the power, like he did for me, to *never, never give up!*

Now, in the next chapter, I want to share with you about one of the greatest miracles I have ever seen in my whole life. As a mother or father, can you imagine anything worse than being told by doctors that your handsome little boy should be institutionalized?

But God had the last word, and this momma bear was not about to give up on her boy!

8

Chipping Away at the Mountain

My Miracle Boy

I knew something wasn't right with my second pregnancy. In the womb, my baby boy moved constantly, kicking and kicking, as though he were in some kind of turmoil.

I prayed and dedicated him to the Lord, but after he was born, weighing nine pounds, he still squirmed and kicked restlessly. And when the nurse placed him on the warming table, he raised himself up, which was very abnormal. At that age, a newborn can't even roll over, much less raise himself up. I yelled when I saw the nurse leave his side, knowing he might roll or push himself off the table.

A few years later, my son, Cameron, had not improved, so my doctor sent me to a neurologist, whom he said was "the best pediatric neurologist in this hemisphere." When the neurologist examined Cameron, who was now three years old, he called in a few other specialists. Finally, he said to me, "Mrs. Raschke, I have some bad news. . . "

I braced myself, knowing something was terribly wrong.

"Your son has the worst case of ADHD (Attention Deficit Hyper-Activity Disorder) I have ever seen." Furthermore, the child psychologist said he has a severe case of ODD (Oppositional Defiant Disorder). He warned that Cameron would grow so huge and his brain would be so full of activity, that he would probably hurt other children.

He also had CAPD (Central Auditory Processing Development Disorder), which meant he could not express himself verbally in a way to be understood.

What the doctor told me next almost caused my heart to stop beating. Both my pediatrician and the neurologist said, "Cameron needs to be put on heavy medication and placed in an institution. But if you decide to keep him at home, you must remove your daughter, Diona, from the home, to keep her from getting hurt."

I was heartsick. At first, shock and grief almost paralyzed me. I could never give up my precious Diona, now six years old, to protect her from my son. *Never!* But neither would it be possible to tear away my son and place him in an institution. *That would be impossible! I absolutely refused to give up!*

Then suddenly I felt that little twinge of hope, that

tiny flame of faith. I focused on that flame until it glowed brighter and hotter within me. As faith rose up, I finally blurted out, "No, Devil! You will not destroy my family! You will not divide us. You will not take my son! And you will not remove my daughter!"

By now I was shaking with the fierceness of a momma grizzly who would not allow her cubs to be ripped from her side. When they told me what I must do, I said, "Hell no!" I meant literally—"No to hell!" The evil spirits were coming for my boy, and I would fight them with all the might of heaven.

Jeremiah said, "'Is not my word like a fire?' declares the Lord, 'and like a hammer which shatters a rock?'" (Jer. 23:29). The Lord taught me how to pray the Word and how to use it like a sword and a hammer to defeat the enemy.

He showed me to use Cameron's name in the Bible verses. So I would say, for example, Isaiah 54:17: "No weapon that is formed against Cameron shall prosper, and every tongue that shall rise against Cameron in judgement he shall show to be in the wrong."

2 Timothy 1:7 in the Amplified says, "For God did not give Cameron a spirit of timidity (of cowardice, of craven and cringing and fawning fear), but [He has given Cameron a spirit] of power and of love and of calm and

well-balanced mind and discipline and self-control."

I prayed, "Cameron can do all things through Christ which strengthens him" (Phil. 4:13, KJV). Often, I cried out, "Cameron has the mind of Christ" (Phil. 2:5, 1 Cor. 2:16). It was sheer hand-to-hand combat, but I was determined.

When Cameron went to pre-school, most of the teachers understood that he had a brilliant mind with a high IQ, but because he couldn't express himself the way he wanted, people rarely knew how gifted he was.

When he started kindergarten, he still struggled with some of his teachers, but Mrs. Holt had been my daughter's teacher, so she wanted to help work with me and Cameron. Though others said he should be in Special Education classes, Cameron actually qualified for a program which allowed him to stay in regular classes, starting in the first grade.

He loved Mrs. Holt's class. And though he was huge, bigger than all the other students, she made him feel normal. A few years later, when he was in the fifth grade, he accidentally broke a child's leg, because it was hard for him to gauge his strength. But still, Cameron was doing so much better.

One day, seven teachers from all of Cameron's classes wanted to meet with me. They had reviewed his file and said, "Mrs. Raschke, we have read all his files, and we cannot believe he is the same boy. We don't want these files to follow him into high school. We want him to have a clean record."

Can you believe it? Cameron's file was wiped perfectly clean. I said to those dear teachers, "Would you like to know how this happened? It was prayer and the Word of God." I showed them some of the scriptures I had been praying, and they were deeply touched. But isn't that just like Jesus? Because of His sacrifice on the cross, His blood wipes the slate clean and gives us a fresh start.

When the seventh-grade football coach saw Cameron, he blurted, "I want *him!*" We had always taught Cameron to be gentle with people, and now he had to re-learn a different concept for the rough-and-tumble game of football.

A few years passed, and now my son entered high school with no record whatsoever of his previous struggles. He had a clean slate, and the coaches were thrilled to see him walk through the front door of the school at 6'5" and 330 pounds!

He became very popular. And when other football teams had to play Kerrville, they all dreaded having to face Cameron Raschke!

When I stopped and thought of all that God had done

in the last sixteen years, I was overwhelmed at the goodness and faithfulness of God.

Colleges around the country sought after him, offering scholarships and full rides. He accepted a full scholarship plus one year in a master's degree program at University of Texas at El Paso.

You see, the enemy wanted to paralyze me with fear, but God wanted to make me into a fierce warrior. He wanted to teach me how to hammer down the mountain with God's Word.

Every day I chipped away at that granite mound of ADHD with verses of faith about Cameron. I bashed and battered that stone precipice until I saw it begin to crumble and fall into the sea.

The Bible says that angels are spirit messengers sent by God to serve us (Heb. 1:14). Psalm 103:20 says that angels wait to obey the voice of God's Word. That tells me that angels will work on our behalf, but they are waiting for us to pray His Word so they can "obey the voice of His Word."

I tell you, I pummeled that snowy peak of ODD until it gradually began to melt. I clobbered that massive heap of CAPD with verses that spoke of God's power and ability to overcome until it, too, began to be crushed and ground into powder (see Appendix for more of these Scriptures).

I felt like Eleazar, one of David's mighty warriors, who "stood his ground and struck down the Philistines till his hand grew tired and froze to the sword" (2 Samuel 23:10 NIV). God's Word was my sword, and I refused to let go until I saw the mountain "cast into the sea" (Mark 11:22-23).

Cameron finished his master's degree and then earned his doctorate in physical therapy. Today he is a physical therapist and owns his own clinic. Of course, it would be impossible to describe this momma's pride in her son and my gratitude to my God for all He did for him. My son and I are still close today, and we can talk about anything. But let me tell you now about one of my sweetest moments.

I had been invited to tell my story on TBN (Trinity Broadcasting Network) several times, but once Cameron and I were on the program together. After I told about the prayer battle I fought for my son, Cameron turned to me and, before God and all the television viewers, he said, "Mom, I love you so much. Thank you for being such a wonderful mom!"

To be a little girl who grew up practically motherless, with no one to fight for me when I was being so abused, caused my heart to fill with measureless love and gratitude to God for His gracious miracle. He is the God of the impossible, and Cameron truly is my miracle boy.

~

So now, let me ask you—what impossible mountains block your path? Maybe a doctor has told you there is no hope, but remember, God has the last word.

Perhaps your child is far away from the Lord. Maybe you are facing an impossible situation of some kind. Whatever your mountain is, bring it to the cross and chip away at the mountain with the jackhammer of God's Word and the power of the blood of the Lamb. Then watch as your mountain crumbles into a molehill and slips slowly into the sea.

Let me tell you now about a trial that the Holy Spirit asked me to walk through. It was so incredibly difficult that I could have been tempted to give up. But the Holy Spirit showed me that I must *never, never give up*, for He would carry me through.

And in the midst of it, He sent me my own personal Florence Nightingale—my own beloved daughter. Diona and I already had a strong bond, but this made us even closer. It created an unshakable mother-daughter relationship that I will treasure forever. . .

9

Life's Unexpected Interruptions

Diona—My Florence Nightingale

I want to tell you now about one of life's unexpected interruptions. But what I most want to tell you is about my incredible daughter, Diona, who stood with me every step of the way.

It all began on a crisp autumn day. Golden leaves fell from the trees outside my window as my daughter Diona and I waited for the phone call from the doctor. The Lord had already told me about something that would be coming, but He promised, "I will be with you whatever you walk through." Again He said, "I will be with you, whatever you walk through, I will be with you."

I knew something was up because I had already had a mammogram, then a follow up ultrasound, and finally a biopsy. Now Diona and I sat together in my sanctuary, the special room in my house dedicated for prayer. It was so comforting to have her there with me.

Finally, the phone rang and I put it on speakerphone. The doctor said, "I'm so sorry to have to tell you this, but you do have invasive ductal carcinoma, in other words, breast cancer."

Diona and I just looked at each other. I said, "O-kaaay . . ." Because the Lord had already prepared me, I wasn't surprised, but I felt numb. When I hung up, Diona said softly, with tears in her eyes, "I'm so sorry, Mom. . . but we will get through this together."

We hugged and tears flowed freely. I felt so supported and loved by my beautiful daughter. But before I tell you the rest of my story, I want you to know the back-story of how, even before she was born, I almost lost my precious Diona.

I was only 21 when doctors found a tumor in my sinus cavity. This required immediate surgery, but on the day I went for my pre-op x-ray, the technician asked if I could be pregnant. I said, "No, I don't think so." But just to be safe, she placed a shield around me before the x-ray.

Then she told the surgeon, "Louada really needs a blood test before you inject the dye for the arteriogram test." I didn't know that this dye, which helps the surgeon identify what kind of tumor it is, could cause serious birth defects or even kill a baby.

As a precaution, the doctor ordered a blood test to determine pregnancy. We waited for the test results and he came back in, saying, "Well, Louada, get dressed!" I was startled, but then he explained, "You are pregnant! You go home now, and we will watch the tumor and operate on it after the baby is born."

I was shocked to know I was pregnant, but incredibly thankful to God that both the technician and the doctor had taken those safety measures. Within twenty-four hours, the dye he would have injected in my groin would have killed my baby or left her with serious birth defects.

When I realized how close we came to almost losing Diona, it took my breath away. I cannot imagine my life without my baby girl. I thank God for His timely intervention.

When it was finally time for her to be born, she didn't come on the due date. My momma kept telling me, "Diona will not be born until my birthday!" A few days later, my labor started. It was June 24 and guess what? That was my momma's birthday!

I hadn't been at the hospital long before I heard my momma coming down the hospital hallway, squealing in a high-pitched voice, "I told you she would be born on my birthday!"

And when Momma held my firstborn baby girl, the look on her face was like a sunrise. She smiled from ear to ear. Momma had become a new creation in Christ, and this baby, born on her birthday with black hair just like hers, was a special love-kiss from Jesus.

Now the years had passed, and here we were embracing, as Diona, now a grown woman, comforted me in my time of trial. I so needed her in that moment and in the days to follow.

Diona and Sean and their two precious children, Zayne and Emma, would all move in with us to take care of me. They were all such a blessing.

One day, before they came, the devil whispered to me, "You are going to die!" Immediately, it came up out of my spirit, "Devil you can't threaten me with heaven! And by the way, whether I live on earth or die and go to heaven, *I win!* You don't!"

I knew, however, that this could not be my time to die. God had spoken to me clearly at twelve years old and promised, "I have called you to preach and teach and minister in music all over the world." I had not done that yet, so I knew I would live and not die, and I would continue to declare the works of the Lord!

Soon two breast surgeries had been performed, followed by six months of chemo and then radiation. The chemo was difficult; that's why, before every insertion of the chemical, I would always say, "Wait just a minute; I need to pray over this: 'Lord, I pray that this chemo will only do good and not harm.'" I think this was a testimony to the attending nurses and patients.

However, I did start losing my hair. I'm sure you can imagine how difficult this would be for any woman. Now I kept seeing my long, blond hair on my pillow, on the floor, and the chair where I read my Bible.

Referring to the scripture that says a woman's hair is her glory (1 Cor. 11:15), I asked, "Lord, will I lose my glory?" He responded, "No, I will be your glory!"

Finally, I decided that the best thing to do would be to shave my head. As my long-time friend, Callie Lutz, came over to start shaving, she looked in my eyes and swallowed hard. I nodded for her to go ahead. Afterward, I looked in the mirror and burst into tears. I needed to let that grief out over the loss of my hair, but then the Lord said, "Will you go without a head covering?"

He told me that if I kept my head bare, it would be an amazing witnessing tool. He said it would be like a magnet, drawing people to me from everywhere.

I prayed with many people in the chemo waiting room. I cried for my friends who had worse cancer than me. I would see the tears in their eyes, and it would break my heart. But I prayed for them with all my might, and they were always grateful.

Once I hurried through a grocery store when a little boy said, "Hi! I just went to the doctor for my ear." As I walked down the aisle, he shouted, "I love you!"

"Well, I love you, too!" I responded. As I thought about how sweet that little incident was, the Lord said, "I just wanted to tell you I love you!"

Through it all, Diona was always there for me. She cooked for me, she cleaned, she brought me shakes and supplements. She was there day and night. She always went with me to every treatment. And on top of that, my son-in-law and grandkids were a tremendous help, too.

I was incredibly grateful that so many people reached out to me, bringing gifts and food and prayers and helping with my GoFundMe account, which my dear friend Teresa Chittenden set up on Facebook.

There were those who asked, "Why didn't you trust God and let Him heal you?" All I know is—the Lord himself directed me to take chemo and radiation, and I knew I had heard from Him. Of course, I knew God could heal me miraculously, but I didn't know that a whole harvest field of souls awaited me in that chemo room.

It wasn't lack of faith. It was mature faith, which follows whatever God says. He said to take the treatments, so I obeyed. Yes, to be sure it was a painful crucible, but it seemed to be a testimony to so many people. After six months of chemo and 21 radiation treatments, I felt exhausted and weak, but full of faith.

And above all, the most precious part was the way my daughter supported and comforted and loved me through it all. She always put my needs above her own. She was selfless and caring and constantly supportive. She was my rock. She was my hero, my own personal Florence Nightingale, who founded modern nursing. Yet I knew she was dealing with her own emotions about possibly losing her mom.

There were times I felt so weak I could only whisper, "Jesus, Jesus, Jesus." The hardest part of all was that my forty-year marriage was falling apart. While in the midst of my suffering, I watched it crumble before my eyes.

When it finally ended, my heart was completely shattered. I have never been so broken. I felt like I had been crushed to powder. I wept and wept, sobbing and wailing, but I knew it was over. I felt like my life was over, too. I was almost ready to give up, but God began to heal my heart and give me the oil of joy for mourning.

As soon as I was able, I was back on my feet ministering to other broken people.

∼

Are you enduring some kind of physical suffering? Are you going through chemo and losing your hair? Do you feel forsaken by a husband or wife or even God?

I can promise you this—Jesus will never ever forsake you. Lean on Him and let Him be your healer and your comforter. Honestly, I have seen more healing miracles than I can even count, but sometimes we do face unexplainable interruptions. This is when we must cling tightly to His cross and *never, never give up!*

And that is exactly where we will go in the next chapter. I can't wait to show you, like you've probably never seen before, what Jesus did for you when He was your substitute Lamb on the cross. This will show you how profoundly Jesus really loves you.

Turn the page and you will discover the greatest victory ever seen in heaven or earth. This is the secret of my whole life. I like to call it "God's Rescue Mission. . ."

10

God's Rescue Mission
The True Secret of My Life

My heart trembled as I stood high on the windswept hill, at the foot of the seven-story "Empty Cross." I felt so honored that God had asked me to minister on Resurrection Morning at this hallowed place.

This was The Coming King Sculpture Prayer Garden, created by Max Greiner, Jr. along with his wife Sherry. Once a rocky barren hillside, it was now a lovely garden on top of a hill outside Kerrville in the hill country of Texas.

Here I stood, once a broken, abused little girl, now standing tall and whole and resonating with the anointing of the Holy Spirit. I knew with all my heart that my healing had come through the finished work of Jesus on the cross. That's why the cross is the true secret of my life.

My thoughts slipped back to that sacred event long ago on another hill outside a city—the hill of Calvary outside the city of Jerusalem. I lifted up my voice to the crowd of spiritually hungry people surrounding me. I could feel the passion rising in my heart as I cried, "We are here to celebrate the greatest event in all human history—the death, burial, and resurrection of Jesus Christ!"

The people responded with shouts of joy. I took a deep breath and looked around. This was not a typical Resurrection Morning. We were all wrapped in coats as the blustering clouds hid the sun and painted the sky gray. Gusts of cold wind blew over the hillside, but I was determined not to let the weather dampen the powerful message the Holy Spirit had given me.

I didn't realize then how desperately we all needed this message of hope. In only nine months the whole planet would be struck by a worldwide pandemic, and unknown to me, in just seven months, I would receive the phone call telling of the cancer in my body. This message of Christ and Him crucified was urgently needed for all of us.

With excitement and fervor, I cried, "I am here today to tell you about 'God's Rescue Mission'—the greatest mission ever performed on the face of the earth! It began over 2,000 years ago and is still going on today."

The yearning on people's faces drew out my passion like a magnet. So I said, "Our story begins in the Garden of Gethsemane, which is an enclosed olive orchard on the Mount of Olives. This was a fitting place for Jesus to pray because this was where olives were crushed to press out the oil. And of course, the oil is a symbol of the Holy Spirit and the anointing.

"Here in the garden, we get a small glimpse of what Jesus was about to endure so that He could rescue us. He said, 'My soul is sorrowful to the point of death' (see Matt 26:38). Have any of you ever been there? I have a few times but nothing like this.

"Then 'He went a little farther and fell facedown and prayed, My Father, if—*IF*—it is possible, let this cup pass from me!' (see Matt 26:39). Luke explains that 'in His anguish, He was praying fervently; and His sweat was like drops of blood falling down on the ground'" (see Luke 22:44).

I shuddered at the thought and said, "I've never prayed that hard, but Jesus did. Why then did He spill His own blood, even before the cross? Was He afraid to die? *No, of course not!*

"The Bible says, 'For He made Him who knew no sin to be made sin for us so that we might become the righteousness of God' (see 2 Cor. 5:21). Jesus shrank from the horror of becoming sin, but even more—He cringed from the terror of drinking the Father's cup, which would demolish sin.

"What then was in this cup, which caused the blood to squeeze out from the pores of His skin? The answer is almost unthinkable. . .

"It was God's cup of wrath and divine judgment against sin, which He must fully drink. Now let me read to you this quote from Dr. Sandy's book *UNDONE by a Revelation of the Lamb:*[1]

> It wasn't just the pain of nails and scourge and spear! It wasn't only the dread of rejection and the terror of bearing our sin! Above all else, it was the horror of enduring floods and floods of God's wrath and punishment against our sin! This is what the Father showed Him in the great Covenant of Redemption before the creation of the world! This is what caused Him to bellow that cry, 'My God, my God, why have You forsaken me?' on the cross."[2]

I sighed heavily and said, "You see, He bore the weight of *every single sin* that I have ever committed or ever will commit, every sin of omission or commission, *every single one of my sins*, which would have been enough to crush Him.

"But add to that my family, the sin of you and your family—*every single sin*. And what about in our city, in our region, in our state, in the United States—He would carry *every single sin* to the cross.

"In fact, every single person alive on the face of the planet—He bore their sin, even though they may not have even been born yet (see Romans 3:25). But most of all, He paid the price to rescue us. He bore the wrath and punishment of God for *every single sin* of all humanity. Can you imagine the weight and the crushing?"

By now my face burned, tears swam in my eyes, and my voice vibrated. "Oh, the crushing! Oh, the pain! Oh, the suffering! Now do you see? That's why He sweat great drops of blood in the garden. This is the agony He experienced so that He could pay the price for our sin and rescue you and me.

"That's why He said to Peter, when he whipped out his sword and cut off Malcus' ear, 'Put your sword away, Peter. Am I not to drink the cup the Father has given Me to drink?' (see John 18:11). This verse shows us that the cup He would drink is not called Jesus' cup, not the Holy Spirit's cup, this is called 'the Father's cup.'

"Thus Jonathan Edwards, who is considered by many scholars as America's greatest theologian, said, 'His principal errand for coming to earth was to drink that cup.'"[3]

Now the crowd could no longer hold back. They began clapping and openly responding to the shock of what Jesus did for them.

I continued, "Isaiah 53:6 says, 'The Lord has laid on Him the iniquity of us all.'" Suddenly, my voice rose higher, compelled by the power of the Holy Spirit surging within me, for this was His message, not mine.

"He paid the total price for our total salvation. He didn't do a halfway job. He didn't stop in the garden where great drops of blood soaked his robe. He didn't say, 'That's enough, I can't bear anymore!' He paid the complete price for all the sins of all humanity. He didn't stop short. Why? Because He *loves us so much!*"

Now my voice was shaking so hard I thought I would burst out crying. But I felt such a blaze in my heart that I kept on earnestly preaching.

"I want you to be impressed today, not by me because I am not impressive, but to be impressed by the sacrificial love of the Lord Jesus Christ for you! Hallelujah! What a price! What a suffering! What a grief! What an agony—all for love!

"You know the Passover was a type of the cross (see 1 Cor. 5:7). He was our Passover Lamb, roasted over the fire of God's wrath even as the lamb was roasted over the fire. Think of it, when we confess our sin and earnestly receive Christ, our sin is passed over. But it's not enough to *know* He fully drank the Father's cup of wrath and fiery judgment. You must *believe* it and *accept* it, which is so much more than just knowing about it."

I paused and said, "Consider how much He endured for you and me. He was the *innocent* Lamb of God. He was rejected; He was insulted and spit upon; He was beaten by the Roman scourge, a whip with bits of bone and jagged metal and heavy weights so that it would dig down deep into His tissue and bone. Fragments of flesh were torn from His body so that He was 'unrecognizable as a man' (see Isa. 52:14).

"A twisted crown of thorns was shoved down on His head and a mock scepter jammed into His hand. Then Roman soldiers beat Him in the head, battering the thorns into His skull. Spikes were driven through His hands and feet. Not little nails—spikes! He had to push himself down on the spikes in His feet to lift His lungs for air.

"By now the darkness had fully shrouded the land. A spear was driven through His side from which blood and water poured. Most scholars believe that His heart ruptured or in essence exploded.

"Yes, His heart broke for you! For 'God so loved the world that He gave His one and only Son that whoever believes in Him can have everlasting life' (see John 3:16).

"Jesus gave His all. He was our substitute. He chose to pay the price for your redemption from drugs and alcohol and adultery and all of our sin. He willingly laid down His life. And be assured—the devil didn't take it from Him!

"He released His spirit to the Father and slowly bowed His head. What happened next is astounding. Over in the temple the veil tore in two from top to bottom, signifying that Jesus, whose flesh is the veil (Heb 10:19) was torn in two on the cross. Now the way into the Holy of Holies is open for you and me."

I sighed and smiled as joy swept through the crowd. Then I shouted, "Now we can go right into the presence of God. Now we don't have to go through a priest or a man. The Father tore the veil because the veil of His Son was torn. And you can go straight in because of the blood of Jesus."

By now the people were so overwhelmed they could hardly stop clapping. It's not that they had never heard this before; it's that now the truth was penetrating their hearts. They told me later that they had never heard such preaching. Or if they had, it had been a long, long time.

Faith and authority rose higher in my heart, and I shouted, "Suddenly, there was an earthquake and the rocks cracked open. IT WAS EARTH-SHAKING. IT ROCKED THE WORLD AND IT'S STILL ROCKING THE WORLD TODAY! I'M TELLING YOU—JESUS CHRIST CHANGED THE WHOLE WORLD!

"You see, this is why Jesus is the secret and purpose of my life. He is fully God and fully Man. He was punished for my sin and yours, but then on the third day, He broke through the bonds of death and rose from the grave. That's why there is salvation in no other name—not

Mohammed, not Buddha, not New Age. No one but Jesus can save you!

"So I am telling you today, you must be born again before you can enter the kingdom of God. You must have a living, breathing, close relationship with Him. You must have a walking, talking intimacy with Him. Oh, friends, do you see why we have to get back to preaching Jesus Christ and Him crucified?

"Listen to me. Jesus is coming again. Paul said:

> For the Lord himself shall come down from heaven with a shout, with the voice of the archangel and the blast of the shofar. And the dead in Christ shall rise first. Then we who are alive, who are left behind, will be caught up together with them in the clouds, to meet the Lord in the air—and so we shall ever be with the Lord" (1 Thess. 4:16-17).

My time was up, so I ended with this final proclamation: "Jesus is the Lamb that was slain from the foundation of the world! He is the Lamb that was slain, and He is now the Lamb who has risen and sits upon the throne!"

The people exploded with shouting and clapping, knowing they had experienced an encounter with the living God here at the foot of the "Empty Cross." All glory and honor to Jesus and Him alone!

That's why I can tell you that when God sent down His one and only Son, this was indeed His divine Rescue Mission. I know because He rescued me, and this is the secret and purpose of my life.

~

So now, if you feel like I do, all you can do is kneel and worship. He is holy, He is worthy, He is deserving of all our praise forever and ever, Amen!

ENDNOTES:

[1] Sandy Davis Kirk, *UNDONE by a Revelation of the Lamb* (Lake Mary, FL: Creation House, 2013).

[2] Sandy Davis Kirk, *UNDONE by a Revelation of the Lamb*, p. 10.

[3] Jonathan Edwards, "Christ's Agony," *The Works of Jonathan Edwards*, Vol 1 (Edinburgh, Scotland: Banner of Truth Trust, 1995), p. 868.

11

Never Give Up
on Your Calling

Yielding to the Holy Spirit

On the day when the Holy Spirit filled me, He changed everything for me. He gave me the boldness to confront my abusers, and they ran like scared rabbits.

He gave me the courage to sing "One Day at a Time" in church, and though I trembled like a leaf in a storm, the Holy Spirit came down with such power on the people that I was forever consumed by His anointing.

He told me I would preach and teach and minister in music all over the world. Then He taught me how to play the second-hand piano that Marvis, my mentor, gave me. I couldn't read music, but He taught me how to *feel* it. I could sense the chords. My spirit would resonate with the presence of God when I would lose myself in worship and rise into the heights of heaven.

Soon I was leading worship in many different venues, and it was glorious. Nothing thrilled me more than when chaos was erupting all around me, and I would steal away to lift my heart and worship Jesus.

Not only did the Holy Spirit give me the power to break the threat of alcoholism off my life, which the devil had planned for me, but He gave me the grace to break the power of alcoholism and addiction and abuse off my whole family. Now my uncle is saved; my momma is saved; my children are saved, and the generational curse of alcoholism and addiction is broken off my children and my grandchildren.

Furthermore, God gave me the wisdom, understanding, and direction to break off the incest, the abuse, and the violence from my family. I took authority in the power of Jesus' name and the victory of His blood over these evil forces that had ruled for generations in my family. And the Holy Spirit himself showed up.

This little girl, who was so afraid of everything and would never sing or preach or even open her mouth in school, now leads worship and teaches and preaches the Gospel on radio and television which reaches all over the world. What the devil meant for evil, God has turned for good.

Now, before you close this book, I want to call you to *never, never give up!* Jesus didn't give up when He saw what was in the Father's cup and blood exuded from the pores of His skin in the garden; He didn't give up when they scourged Him and crushed Him with thorns; He didn't give up when they spiked Him up to two stakes of wood.

And most of all, He didn't give up when He bore your sin and engulfed every last drop of the Father's cup. He never gave up in the midst of His most horrific trial, and He calls you to *never, never give up* but to lean on Him for the rest of your life on earth.

~

Yes, once upon a time, a desperate little girl, in the midst of catastrophic danger, whose mother had passed out at the wheel of her speeding car, cried out to a God she didn't know. Thinking her momma had turned into a monster, she screamed from the depths of her being, *"Father!"*

From that point on, her life began to slowly change. I know because I was that little girl. I am living proof that God can change a busted and broken life. He did it for me; He will do it for you.

So, like that little girl long ago, cry out to Him with all your heart—*"Father!"* Then yield yourself to the Holy Spirit, and *never, never, never give up on His calling in your life!*

ACKNOWLEDGMENTS

First, I thank You, Heavenly Father, for rescuing a little abused girl that was full of fear, rejection, and shame. I had no future, no hope. I would have surely gone the way of those in my family that were bound by heavy chains of addictions. You stepped in and rescued me. Gave me a future and a hope. You spoke and showed me that I was full of value and worth. You truly saved me in every sense of the word.

Thank you, Lord, that I have been commissioned to preach the wonderful news of the glory of the exalted God. My heart spills over with thanks to God for the way He continually empowers me, and to our Lord Jesus, the Anointed One, who found me trustworthy and who authorized me to be His partner in this ministry (1 Timothy 1: 11-12, TPT). I am so humbled, Lord, that You would choose me to tell others about You and how wonderful You are!

To my daddy, Jack Turner—thank you for always believing in me and thinking I walk on water! Well, I know that is not true, but it sure is nice you think it is. You are by far the greatest man I have ever known! Your love, support, and encouragement means so much. Thank you for your advice and wisdom through the years. Knowing you faithfully pray for me means more than I can put in words. God broke the mold when He created you. There is no one like you in all the world!

To my family: Diona, Sean, Zayne, Emma Montgomery, and Cameron Raschke—you are so much of my story and who I am. Having you in my life is one of the highest honors that could ever be given to me. Being your mom, mother-in-law, and Grammy is such an amazing blessing! Each of you are a joy and delight to my heart. Oh, how I treasure you. Thank you for standing with me and believing in the call of God upon my life.

Donna and David James—you have been in my life since I was fourteen. You have been prayer warriors and intercessors for me. You have ministered alongside of me for years. You are my friends and family. You have helped mold and train me for the call of God upon my life. You have blessed and helped my family countless times. You have been such a support to me and the ministry. You have gone over and above the call of duty. God put us together, and nothing has ever stopped that. So glad we have done life together all these years.

Teresa Chittenden—words fail me. How can I ever describe how much our over-35-year-long friendship has meant to me? You are so much a part of my life. You are my 3:00 a.m. friend who I can call when my life is completely turned upside down and know will be on the other end. You have been by my side and walked with me through the fire. You have encour-aged, counseled and mentored me. We have prayed together and cried together. Our families have been intertwined through all these years. You and Steve have done so much for us. Money could never repay, words would never be adequate. I appreciate you so and don't ever want to do life without you. Thank you!

Jeff and Dawn Kanady—you have been my close, precious friends and co-laborers in the ministry for many, many years. You have stood and stood and stood with me. We have been through a lot together. You served alongside me for decades when there was not a penny to be had for anything. You stayed the course. You held up my arms. You encourage me. You keep me from getting lost! You help me with practical things as well as ministry. You do things with excellence and integrity. We work hard together, and we have fun together! Thank you for being my friends first, then ministry partners. I could not even begin to imagine doing ministry or life without you in it. I can't wait to see all that the Lord has in store for us. We make a great team!

Dr. Sandy Kirk—you took me by the hand and walked me through the writing of my life's story. You are an anointed, accomplished author of 31 published books. Your revelation of the Father's cup and the cross of Christ have powerfully impacted me and so many others. Yet, you took the time out of your own busy schedule to teach and co-write WITH me. So amazing! You saw God in my story and declared it needed to be told to encourage and give hope to others. I have enjoyed this process with you, even the editing, timelines and fact checks! I have learned much from you that I believe will carry over into future books that I will write. You masterfully brought my story "out" of me. You could have taken the stories and facts of my life and written it all by yourself. Instead, you used my own words and wove them together with yours into a flowing, exciting, easy-to-read book. I am so honored and blessed by your generosity, Dr. Sandy. You have given me the gift of your time, talent and experience. Thank you from the bottom of my heart for helping make my story come to life in a book. A dream come true! Thank you for working selflessly and tirelessly on this project. Most of all, thank you for being my friend.

Pat Parker—you have blessed me so much through the years. I am thankful God put you in my life when I was fourteen. You have faithfully prayed for me. You have been a confidante. When times were rough you were there for me and our family. You encouraged me and prayed with me and gave me godly advice. You are my friend and family.

Dianna Holloway—you have a way of edifying me and lifting me up in the Spirit. You are always so very encouraging. Your confidence in who God is in me truly blesses me and builds my faith. I am so thankful for you and for God bringing you into my life when I was fourteen. You are my friend and family.

Jack and Carol Rothenflue—apparently, I still need mentors even at my age, because that is what you are to me. I have great respect for who you are in the Spirit. Your words carry weight with me. You have given me wisdom and wise counsel from the Lord many times. You helped me during the most crushing experience of my life, and you continue to be there for me. You have been able advocates for me before the throne of God. I just want you to know how much you mean to me. I am so grateful you are in my life.

To my Pillars of Prayer (POP) Ladies—your faithful intercession has held me and strengthened me. It has brought me through rough waters. Your powerful prayers have been the undergirding strength needed to do the work of the Lord. Without you, I cannot fulfill the call to preach, teach and minister in music all over the world. You are an integral, extremely important part. Together we will minister to the multitudes!

Pat Jordan—thank you for being a wise counsel for me so many times as a young woman, wife, and mother. You were a shoulder to cry on. You listened and prayed. You were a godly mentor and friend. You tried to teach me how to cook, LOL! It didn't take, but I sure loved to eat your cooking! You and Lyle made an impact on me that I carry to this day.

James and Patsy Durst—you have prayed for me year after year (actually, since I was seventeen!). You believed in the call upon my life from the moment I met you. You encouraged me to pursue it. You were a listening ear and a word of wisdom when I needed it. Your prophetic words from the Lord to me were always timely. Thank you for being there for me!

Irene Long—I am so thankful you took a chance on me nearly 40 years ago. You hired me for a job for which I had no experience. Although I only worked there a few years, our friendship remains strong to this day. Thank you for your faithful prayers and friendship.

Polly and Jay Kinsel—thank you for your friendship and all the ways you helped me in the ministry and personally all those years. I appreciate all of the support and encouragement you gave me!

Pastor David, Cindy Danielson, and Impact Church—thank you for your prayers and believing in the call upon my life. You have encouraged me to be the "me" that God created. I love your kingdom-mindedness. I am filled up at every church service. I love the Word and worship that comes forth Sunday after Sunday at Impact. Thank you for all you do for Him and His people!

Pastor Del and Cindy Way—thank you for believing in the call of God upon my life and ordaining me years ago. What a blessing that was and is. Thank you for not only taking me to record my "YOUR LOVE" CD but for paying for the entire project! What an honor it was for me to record some of your songs on it that you wrote, Pastor Del. I am forever grateful!

AGLOW International—you have been an important part of my life for many decades. You have been a source of training, teaching, and support. You believed in me and what God was doing in my life. You allowed me to minister in the Word and music in the early years up to the present. It is one of the greatest blessings and honors of my life. You have helped train me for the Great Commission. I love serving with you all. Ms. Carol Torrance, I love and respect you more than you will ever know!

There are so many others that are a part of my story. There is no way I could name all of you that have been there for me through thick and thin, the good and the bad, over the years. You have mentored, counseled, prayed, supported financially, and ministered with me and to me personally. Some of you have even fed me and my family and helped keep a roof over our heads in the lean years. Know that you are loved, you are appreciated. Each of you are a part of the reward of the harvest from my life and ministry. THANK YOU from the bottom of my heart!!!!!!

APPENDIX

Scriptures I prayed over my children, making it personal and inserting their name:

Josh 24:15 (AMPC) ...as for me and my house, we will serve the Lord.

Acts 16:31 (NKJV) Believe on the Lord Jesus Christ, and you will be saved, you and your household.

Isa 54:13 (AMPC) _____ is a disciple taught by the Lord and obedient to His will, and great shall be the peace and undisturbed composure of _____.

Isa 54:17 (AMPC) No weapon that is formed against _____ shall prosper, and every tongue that shall rise against you in judgment you shall show to be in the wrong.

Isa 50:4-5 (AMPC) [The servant of God says] The Lord God has given _____ the tongue of a disciple and of one who is taught, that _____ should know how to speak a word in season to him who is weary. He wakens _____ morning by morning, He wakens _____ ear to hear as a disciple [as one who is taught]. The Lord God has opened _____ ear, and _____ has not been rebellious or turned backward.

Isa 53:4a (AMPC) Surely He has borne _____ griefs (sicknesses, weaknesses, and distresses) and carried _____ sorrows and pain. . .

Isa 53:5 (AMPC) But He was wounded for _____ transgressions, He was bruised for _____ guilt and iniquities; the chastisement [needful to obtain] peace and well-being for _____ was upon Him, and with the stripes that wounded Him _____ is healed and made whole.

Jer 23:29 (AMPC) Is not My word like fire [that consumes all that cannot endure the test]? says the Lord, and like a hammer that breaks in pieces the rock [of most stubborn resistance] (in _____ life)?

Phil 4:8 (KJV) Finally, brethren, whatsoever things are true, whatsoever things are honest, whatsoever things are just, whatsoever things are pure, whatsoever things are lovely, whatsoever things are of good report; if there be any virtue, and if there be any praise, _____, think on these things.

Phil 4:13 (KJV) _____ can do all things through Christ which strengtheneth _____.

Ro 8:37 (AMPC) Yet amid all these things _____
is more than a conqueror and gains a surpassing victory
through Him Who loved us.

1 Cor 2:16b (AMPC) But _____ has the mind of
Christ (the Messiah) and does hold the thoughts (feelings
and purposes) of His heart.

2 Tim 1:7 (AMPC) For God did not give _____
a spirit of timidity (of cowardice, of craven and cringing
and fawning fear), but [He has given _____ a
spirit] of power and of love and of calm and well-balanced mind and discipline and self-control.

Isa 41:10 (NKJV) Fear not, for I am with _____;
Be not dismayed, for I am _____ God. I will
strengthen _____, Yes, I will help _____,
I will uphold _____ with My righteous right hand.

Psa 37:31 (KJV) The law of _____ God is in
_____ heart; none of _____ steps shall slide.

Pictures of My Family

Me at 12 yrs old

Bill Harrison, my biological dad

My dad Bill in the church
where he led me to the Lord

My momma and daddy right
after they got married

Ministering at an
Aglow Conference

Diona (6 yrs old) and
Cameron (3 yrs old)

Diona and Sean
(My daughter and her husband)

Cameron, my son

Leading worship at The
Coming King Prayer Garden

I am about to preach at the "Empty Cross"

Daddy and me

Right after I lost my hair

Diona and me on
the way to chemo

My half sisters

My momma

Daddy and me

Ministry Information

To connect with Louada Raschke Ministries
& take advantage of our FREE RESOURCES

Louadarministries
TV Programs

louadaraschkeministries

@louadaraschke

Louada Raschke Ministries
Radio Podcasts

Www.louada.org

PO Box 291364
Kerrville, TX 78029

befree@louada.org

Office:
830-315-6233

Call Our Prayer Line: 866-241-0579

To DONATE:

@louada

$louada

@louada

Www.louada.org

ABOUT THE AUTHOR

Louada is an ordained minister and worship leader who grew up in a dysfunctional family riddled with alcoholism, rampant divorce, abuse, depression, strife, and violence. At a very young age, she was engulfed in fear and full of rejection and hopelessness. There were no Christians in her family, but at the age of ten she accepted the Lord as her Savior. God began the process of healing her broken heart and renewing her mind. Satan tried many times to pull her into the generational sins of her family line. Through the study of the Word and prayer, she began to understand that she did not have to follow in the footsteps of those before her. God broke the chains that had Louada bound. God gave her a future and a hope. He called her into the ministry to preach, teach, and minister in music the powerful, life-changing Gospel of Christ that she had experienced firsthand. Her mission is to win the lost, set the captives free from addictions and destructive patterns of thinking and lifestyles, pray for the sick, and equip the church to do the same. Louada is an intense, fervent worshipper of God and loves leading others into His presence.